Poems off the Kitchen Table and Ruby's File

Tom Sheehan

Copyright© 2020 Tom Sheehan

ISBN: 978-93-88319-25-6

First Edition: 2020

Rs. 200/-

Cyberwit.net
HIG 45 Kaushambi Kunj, Kalindipuram
Allahabad - 211011 (U.P.) India
http://www.cyberwit.net
Tel: +(91) 9415091004 +(91) (532) 2552257
E-mail: info@cyberwit.net

No part of this book may be reproduced or transmitted in any form or by any means, electronic, mechanical, photocopying, or otherwise, without the express written consent of Tom Sheehan.

Printed at Repro India Limited.

About the author:

Tom Sheehan's *Epic Cures*, (short stories), from Press 53 won a 2006 *IPPY Award from* Independent Publishers. *A Collection of Friends*, (memoirs), 2004 from Pocol Press, was nominated for PEN America Albrend Memoir Award). His fourth poetry book, *This Rare Earth & Other Flights*, issued by Lit Pot Press, 2003. Novels are *Vigilantes East* and *Death for the Phantom Receiver.* and *An Accountable Death.* Seven short story collections have been published. He has nominations for 25 Pushcart Prizes and two Million Writers Awards, a Silver Rose Award from ART for short story excellence, and many Internet appearances. He is a veteran of the Korean War (31st Infantry Regiment), a Boston College graduate after Army service, and has been retired for 23 years.

Contents

A Letter to Orlando 7
Cold Night Thoughts beside an Empty Cave 9
1. Sparrow in the Sierras 10
2. From Nahant, Atlantic Rub, Pacific Skip 11
From Vinegar Hill, A Small Red Star for Me and My Father 12
Late Night Guitar 14
The Sugaring 15
On My Father's Blindness 17
The Municipal Subterranean 19
Night Forgery 20
Once Screamed to the Flag-waving Drunks at the Vets Bar,
Late, Memorial Day Evening 22
Small Influences of Pebbles and Words 26
Mercies Found in Light 28
This House of Ours, 1742 30
A File for Ruby 31
Larkspur 32
Lyrical Vacations North of Boston 39
  I Don't See Too Many Guys in Suntans* Anymore 42
V for Victor 45
Receipt at Ogden's Twist 54
Of Innocence and Reprisal 59
One Orbit Off 65
The Humpty Dumpty Wall 67
Heaven and Hell Have Their Ways 75

A Letter to Orlando

All day the cold is a secret
of my fleece-lined jacket
and the bottom of my mittens.

The senseless wind, without any
direction and purposeless,
gets hung up in the muffler

I wear as some corrective device,
thick and wooly and itchy,
around my neck. It's the one

You left in my van the last winter
we cut wood in Oaklandvale
and waded through a final white tide

Until we fell exhausted.
You used to laugh about wood
heating twice. Now you've gone south,

and only I can hear the cry
of the oak as it lets go
and throws the earth out of kilter.

I walked quietly there yesterday,
snow thrown like paint everywhere
except on the sun side,

Gray birches, easy in the wind,
made me think of Finnish ski troops
the Russians didn't like around.

I suppose there are pieces
of the battlefield left down south,
but I bet you think of here

When a cool wind grabs your neck,
an old jacket lets out secrets,
your fingers remember wood,

And all across a sunset sky,
falling downhill to your ears,
a chainsaw's evening prayers.

Cold Night Thoughts beside an Empty Cave

The pond is hammered
into one piece.
An owl, darkly buried,
carries half the night
away like a canyon
carries an echo down.

When the final touch
is carved on water,
intimately the mouse
knows the owl, and I
am left to the last
enterprise of imagination,
the Christ tree enters
all the shadows.

I am what the Christ tree is,
an upright man at no arms,
a swimmer vertical
in time, elusive saint,
a descendent of Abel
second in the clubbing.

But night and the cold charge
live where the rim hangs
between sunset and sunrise,
halfway into the echo
night carries in its mouth,
a mouse at odds with destiny.

For Stars Not Yet Begun

1. Sparrow in the Sierras

All morning Sparrow moved
above the tree line, hearing only his boots,
loose stones, wind in a bottle in his ear,
a trumpet at odds with the voices he created,
basso profundo; might as well have been opera,
canyon-deep, now and then tenor out of rocks,
ahead, always ahead, calling, promising, whistles
from a formed mouth rocks had made purse-fully
just for the sum of winds
off the peaks, passionate,
moaning as a bride might moan nearing midnight.
For three days, he heard the last word spoken to him,
a quick "g'day" from a prospector passing by as much
apparition as his eyes would allow, swallowed wholly
by a twist in the trail, boots, mule, even the heavy
scent of old burlap and barns and leathers near
destruction fading past recognition, past recall:
Sparrow here, gathering for stars not yet begun.

2. From Nahant, Atlantic Rub, Pacific Skip

For hours he'd been
diving for God knows what, a ballistic bursting air
each time he came up fanning for life, amateur at
what I was good at, surviving, reaching under all
of Neptune it seems.
He brought up a stone, gray,
smooth as the millennium, travel yet indelible, still
worth rubbing, he said when asked. Then, For what?
To August sun he marked it, aloft, victor's clutch,
For the Pacific, he said.
Promising to write, he left,
the stone under denim underway. And this he says:
I did the lakes, the Nations, the high grass for miles,
dry lands, Badlands, the Parks burning for weeks,
false mountains
climbing into Idaho's shadows.
Now, mosquito-ravaged, money gone, tired of the weight
of it all, I have flung it into Alaska's Pacific, rubbed it
one last time for you, that Atlantic charm, drowned it
in water it knew
just ten million years ago before I
came along, Owen McReigghily, biker, Christ-bearded
my own descriptor, who pays no taxes, lives no place
but arbor, dry culvert, waddies back where mountains
have beginnings.
I've done my passage here, freed
Nahant Atlantic's stone to taste new salt. Something
will touch it yet, burn it, shape it, clutch the warmth of
my hands where I rubbed in time,
grind it for stars not yet begun.

From Vinegar Hill, A Small Red Star for Me and My Father

This appointment came when light tired, this arrangement, this syzygy
Of him and me and the still threat of a small red star standing
Some time away at my back, deeper than a grain of memory.
I am a quarter mile from him, hard upward on this rugged rock he could
Look up to if only his eyes would agree once more, and it's a trillion
Years behind my head or a parsec I can't begin to imagine,
They tell me even dead perhaps, that star. Can this be a true syzygy
If one is dead, if one is leaning to leave this line of sight
Regardless of age or love or density or how the last piece of light
Might be reflected, or refused, if one leaves this imposition? The windows
Of his room defer no light to this night, for it is always night there,
Blood and chemicals at warfare, nerve gone, the main one
Providing mirror and lethal lens, back of the eyeball no different
Than out front, but I climb this rock to line up with another rock and him
In the deep seizure of that stolen room, bare sepulcher,
That grotto of mind.

Today I bathed him, the chest like an old model, boned but collapsible,
Forgotten in a Detroit back room, a shelf, a deep closet, waiting
To be crushed at the final blow, skin of the organ but a veneer
Of fatigue, the arms pried as from a child's drawing, the one less formidable
Leg, the small testes hanging their forgotten-glove residuum
Which had begun this syzygy, the face closing down on bone

As if a promise had been made toward an immaculately thin retrieval,
　And, at the other imaginable end of him, the one foot bloody
　　From his curse, soured yet holier in mimicry of the near-Christ
(from Golgotha brought down and put to bed, after god and my father
there are no divinities), toenails coming on a darkness no sky owned,
foot bottom at its own blood bath, at war, at the final and resolute war
　　　　　　　　　　　with no winner.

　Oh, Christ, he's had such wars, outer and inner, that even my hand
　　In warmth must overcome, and he gums his gums and shakes his
　　　　　　　　　　　　　head
　　　And says, sideways, mouth screwed into his outlandish grin,
　　As much a lie as any look, as devious, cold-fact true, "I used to do
　　　　　　　　　　　　this for you,"
　　　The dark eyes hungry to remember, to bring back one moment
　Of all those times to this time; and I cannot feel his hand linger on
　　　　　　　　　　　　　　me,
Not its calluses gone the way of flesh or its nails thicker now than
　　　　　　　　　　　　　　they
Ever were meant to be, or skin flaking in the silence of its dust-borne
　　　　　　　　　　　　　battle,
　　Though we are both younger than the star that's behind us
　And dead perhaps, as said; then, in a moment, and only for a mo-
　　　　　　　　　　　　　ment,
　　As if all is ciphered for me and cut away, I know the failure
　　　Of that small red star, its distillation and spend still undone,
Its yawn red as yet and here with us on the endless line only bent
By my imagination, the dead and dying taking up both ends of me,
　　Neither one a shadow yet but all shadows in one, perhaps
A sort of harmless violence sighting here across an endless known.

Late Night Guitar

I hear an odd wire vibrate
against a dark red wood.

It ripples along, hoarse,
talks a mountain to pieces.

All Iberia is elaborate
in string and lath;

peninsula of high heels,
ribbons dancing on the mane,

black hats horse-parading,
friar's lantern honing swords.

A later moon of Pico de Aneto
dies in the dust of olive trees.

A forlorn SAC bomber, tailed,
falcons its way home silently.

When a bull is born
the earth shakes twice,

and an odd wire vibrates
against a darker red wood.

The Sugaring

My father hid his diabetes
in black shoe tops. At night,
he peeled off bloody socks
where veins found short circuiting.

My mother bought white cotton
socks by the dozens, band aid
throwaways after work or Sunday
best, after his heart pumped

its way down long lean legs
deep Nicaraguan paths had known,
every baseball diamond Boston
shook under red August skies,

who-knows-what in Shanghai.
Later on, it went topsy-turvy
in eyeballs' secret caves,
refracting light into bones,

porous humors going to sponge,
into space where ideas lose out.
When he sat to peel his socks
from their red-wounding rounds,

checking the salvage of the day
like a crow beside the macadam,
or thumbed a Brailled king of
hearts or a diamond five

before he pegged me off the board,
I used to congratulate myself
for not saying anything to him.
He'd shuck off such words just

as he would an uncomfortable
compliment: they paid nothing,
they did nothing, they sat on the
ear like old, old promises.

Just piles of junk, he'd say,
the letter of vocabularies
and sore intentions. Even now,
at cribbage or haberdashery,

seeing apod men humbled to knee,
clothesline flush with socks
as if a semaphore is working,
I remember how he crossed one

leg over the other, fingered
a sock, slowly peeled the skin
away from his angry feet,
casting off evening's surrender flag,

like an Indian, godless, from his coals.

On My Father's Blindness

Time whispered when he had eyes,
a deliberation of things,
songs, stories, a string of beads
some islander made in his equatorial days;

leaves, loaves, salad-making,
great roasts' sizzling songs,

an unhurrying, yieldless time
of games, ghosts, gobs of things.

How when sentences finally came to be,
he read *Cappy Ricks and the Green Pea Pirates*.
His eye on the page, my ear on his tongue,
caesura was a bite of beer, a drink of cheese,
turning words like the roasts he made,
savory succulent tongue,
but page wordless now.

Now! Now!

Now Time strikes!
Hurricanes, lightning, days are crunching,
night is no more a pail of stars
flung as sand on dark skies.
The eyes are closed, the mouth;
when do songs cease to sound?

Sprung from his loins wanting to be,
self-torn from his arms
at some piece of boyhood,
I now remember earless, wordless,
the touch when I was lovely young,

and I know I roam forever
in the darkness of his eyes.

The Municipal Subterranean

He comes up, goggled,
out of a manhole
in the middle of a street
in my peaceful town,
sun the sole brazier,

like an old Saharan
veteran, Rommel-pointing
his tank across the four-
year stretch of sand,
shell holes filling up
quick as death.

I think of Frank Parkinson,
Tanker, Tiger of Tobruk,
now in his grass roots,
the acetylene smile
on his oil-dirty face,
the goggles still high
on his high forehead,
his forever knowing
Egypt's two dark eyes.

Night Forgery

Just before dawn,
a shadow makes tracks
in the dew lit grass.

Later, a whisper
and a scent follow
the forsaken imprints

Not a leaf stirs,
but if I watch closely,
blades of grass ease upright,

a loam granule
is released to airs
staggering under stars,

and the whisper, vague,
is familiar, perhaps stripped
from gists of old conversations.

Years ago,
at a Red Sox game, I
became separated from my father.

All the goblins
of young creation hung over
my hysteria, poked at my terror.

When he found me,
pawed, frayed, diminished,
he said he'd never leave me again.

This soft forging
in the night grass
is a kept word, a vow.

Once Screamed to the Flag-waving Drunks at the Vets Bar, Late, Memorial Day Evening

Fifty years now and they come at me, in Chicago,
Crown Point, Indiana, by phone from Las Vegas.
I tell them how it happened, long after parting, one
night when I was in a bar, thinking of them all.
**

Listen, gunmen,
all I can smell is the gunpowder
on you sharper than booze.
You wear your clothes
with a touch of muzzle flash.

Is it a story you want…?
Listen to the years ago,
to the no shooting,
to the no rout,
to the just dying.

The day stank,
it wore scabs, had odors
to choke tissues and burn
secret laminations of the lungs.
Rain festered in soot clouds,
rose in the Pacific
or the Sea of Japan,
dumped down on us,
came up out of yellow clay
like a sore letting out.

The air must have been
full of bats, of spider weavings;
it was lonely as the lobo,
yet a jungle of minds
filled it with thought leaves
shining with black onyx.

Who needs doctors at dying…?
Prayers sew wounds, piece heads,
hearts, hands together, when blood
and clay strike the same irrevocable
vein, arterial mush; when God
is the earth and clay, silence,
the animal taker leaning to grasp.

Listen, gunmen,
listen you heroes in mirrors
only you see into, we through,
it isn't the killing, it's the dying
must be felt, associated,
even if it stinks.

Blood freezes in hot days
of dying, is icicle inside movement
of trickery less than glacier's,
where a man crawls to his maker
up his own veins, is touched,
feels the firebrand burn in the cold.

Where are the shade trees, cool drinks…?
Once I froze in the confessional
against the fire.

He was a Spick,
they said, washed his skin
too much, wanted to sandpaper it white,
be us, be another man.

But we wagered ourselves
to get him out of a minefield
live as breathing, comrade shot
down in the clay in the rain
in the time of bright eyes rolling
with thunder's fear.

Was it him we carried, or the stone
of his monument…?
Tons he was of responsibility,
one of us despite the Spick name,
man being borne to die.

God is everywhere,
the catechism says, my son says,
now, years later. It was once
a divinity we carried on the poles,
with his balls gone pistonless,
no more a god to his woman.
His image rolled red on the canvas,
burned through the handles of the litter
as secret as electricity; Spick shooting
himself into us, Godhead shooting signs
up shafts of wood.

Lugging God
on sticks and canvas
is frightening. We felt this.

Jesus! We screamed,
have You let go of this god...?
Do You fill him up making him burn
our hands? He wanders now for times,
rolling himself together,
womanless, childless, a journey
in dark trees, among leaves,
in jungles, to get near You.

God seeking God
at the intercept of shrapnel,
the tearing down and lifting up
by our hands, God
in the cement of death.

Oh, gunmen,
it's the dying not the killing
you must speak of. This day
is theirs, not ours, belongs
to the gods of the dead,
of the Spick we carried to his dying
and all his brothers, none of them
here among us.

Drink, gunmen,
one to the Spick and grave's companions,
jungle flights they are in
to match their god with God.

And think, gunmen,
who among us have the longest journey
among leaves, in darkness,
through the spiders of trees,
now.

Small Influences of Pebbles and Words

Even now there are places
where I would drop a pebble,
or a small stone by choice,
gray-blue in sunlight, tumbled

a million years for my hand,
or a word not yet leftover:
into a cave in France to hear
the Preadamites talk again

in the long corridors, their
voices heavy and coarse,
how the day fit for gods
or a tusked pig for firing;

into a mine in the Tetons
cluttered for oblivion,
until I'd hear it clear
the air against water;

into a deserted caisson
under a river where bones
are still perfect in concrete
and timeless rejection;

into a yet-known orifice in
Khirbat Qumran, under sand,
where it might roll a whole
year downward without trick-

ing itself out of the way;
down the cathartic throat
of the editor, who said
the poem had "*To* little sub-
stance, *to* much metaphor."

Mercies Found in Light

Across this newly thickened lake,
my night skates chatter up clouds
of mist as dense as the Milky Way.
Underneath, the fish disbelieve
the sudden hardness of their sky.

It is the darkness makes me love
all the mercies found in light.
Only the blind could love light
more, given one more chance;
a flake of lake ice in their eyes

with a star caught up inside.
If I dare to listen, I hear an event
of ice fracture, a shore to shore
cracking underfoot, schismatic,
a round of forgotten artillery;

or my booted cutlery slashing
lines on the sugar-white surface,
crackling an electricity that divests
thinly clad wire. I am on the lake
after midnight and there is light.

Clarity speaks on cubes of air.
The wind has teeth for the back
of my neck. Only my left arch
is tired, and that from an accident
once on a night moving lightless.

What matters is I am not blind.
Light comes in spheres, or long, thin
lines, in the dusts we know of ex-
plosions. Light is the cold air
sling-shotting pellets at my teeth.

It is what first comes of darkness,
and all the mercies we'll ever know.

This House of Ours, 1742

It is a religion
loving this house,
floors awry, square
nails letting go,
shrieks at night
on footless stairs.

Everything leans
away from fireplaces
in each room, old as
pyramids, and, yet,
still here, like there.

A File for Ruby

Table of Contents and original publication if any

Larkspur/ in A Golden Place, 11/2/09
Lyrical Vacation North of Boston -none
I Don't See Too Many Guys in Suntans Anymore- Facebook 12/4/18
V for Victor-Oddville, 4/30/09
Receipt at Ogden's Twist/ Troubadour 21, 2/18/10
Of Innocence and Reprisal/Troubadour 21, 6/1/10
One Orbit Off/ Troubadour 21, 9/18/10
The Humpty Dumpty Wall, A Golden Place, 9/6/10
Heaven and Hell Have Their Ways

Larkspur

Larkspur knew Katherine loved him in her own a special way, that was a solid given, but as she went out the door that morning, the sun thrusting its divine silhouetted way through her slight and perceivable skirt so that he looked a second time and a third solicitous time with a wide grin. She smiled back at him (really saying, "Time enough for that.") and said, later he thought to be so very casual, "Oh, I forgot to tell you. The water won't go down in the tub. It's probably plugged up. Maybe hair or something like that." ("What else is like hair?" he said to himself, knowing full well from an obvious point of view that she had not shaved 'down there.')

"You should be able to clean it out in a jiffy, hon. I bet the boys will bring some of their pals back from golfing and they might want to use the shower." ("You know darn well they'll be bringing a bunch of pals back and they'll all be showering after the match, and this, I must say, is sandbagging at its best!")

Beyond all his soft appearance, his casual manner in most things ... to be totally truthful, his ineptness in 'most things about the house.' Larkspur loved her fiercely. He loved her in a way she knew she'd never be loved, not on this fair earth, not under cloudy skies or wide and majestic blue that some dawns promised. Not during the finest and deepest snows one could imagine while planked comfortably beside the fireplace, the logs glowing in their own late=night sparkle. Not while the house hove silently into the lovely 'forever,' their two boys and their daughter asleep overhead, his right hand the nerviest and nicest part of his being, in the very beginning, and being foremost in the beginning, a question of innocence.

They both knew she had seduced him, cool, calm and collectedly, brought him from the shell he was, the boy he was, who had looked at her one day in the jammed high school corridor as June madness and vacation crowded down upon them with promise and new freedoms, said with the kindest eyes she had ever seen, with the most honest declaration ever observed, with an unquenchable fire, that he was in love with her now and always would be.

She had latched onto that look, that message, that sudden awareness, and brought it inside of her body, deeply, where it counted, where it flourished continually through to this day.

Each knew he was short on some talents, but with her assistance he did become lord of the manor, as she might have said a hundred times, a thousand times, often in an unabashed and open manner to others in a large gathering. There always was a way to let people know her Larkspur was her one and only lover until the end of time.

But, decidedly, also from the outset, Larkspur was not good at gadgeteering or fixing up the little problems in utilities. Early he had found out that not only was he unaccustomed to gadget innards or their ways of working, but that he was terrified of them and their unholy threats at his balm and serenity. Electric irons terrified him, toasters, televisions, answering machines on the phone, VCRs, electric can openers, pipes and tubes and shut-off valves, solder and brazing, PVC and its special cement, anything that was electrical in nature or called for plumbing or its tools or, further, demanded some ancient knowledge of theory and how elements of 'things' worked in unison with each other for their target use.

Forget automobile engines and attached parts! He was impossible there. That was the sheerest terror of all, out on the byways and highways with the children in the back seat and the hood of the car up as if some ancient tomb was his for history's decoding. Some men, he believed with sincerity, inherited intuitive celerity. It came with their genes. No doubt it was passed down from mechanic to plumber to electrician via little swimming germs with smiling faces and energetic little tails, nestling where they were meant to nestle, deep inside, hidden away, notched, locked, under key, in special cores or places of great reserve where such men 'just knew such things.'

Eventually there came the new onslaught ... the computers and iPads and tablets flat and mysterious and so utterly endless in knowledge and history that they seemingly shoved him into a new place in life, a hollow and mysterious vacuum reserved, he believed, for people just like him.

But, oh, how Katherine protected him in every instance, paring away the mystery that he was in himself, and using it as a lever, a weapon, the armor part of her love that waved for all their years unflaggingly, her eyes in that broadcast too, taking part in her own script, his script.

"Larkspur," Katherine would say, in temperament and support if it were to be balanced at all, "likes to read. And, oh, my God, how he loves postage stamps from all the corners of the Earth and now those from out of space. The great celebrations, the great flights, the sad ones. He has them all ... Shepard, Armstrong, Aldrin, Duke, Glenn, Grissom, Apollo 11, etc., etc., on and on, round and round, whither they go and look back at us from way up there. Larkspur, after all, is a gentleman." Sometimes she said it very formidably, now and then contentedly, occasionally it might drift off to another meaning. That's when Larkspur did not listen, gifted with delicate ears as well as delicate hands.

When Katherine shifted from postage stamps to reading, she had some delicious entries to move into the conversation ..."Can you possibly realize that he twice has read, from first word to last word both times, Kristen Lavransdatter by Sigrid Undset, that great Norwegian epic and Nobel Prize winner, 1600 pages of it. And then, hungry for words and a sense of history and another time, he picked up by chance The Chronicles of Saint Patrick, the Captivity by John Thomas Clark about 5th century

Ireland, over 800 pages, and he still has it at his elbow, that darling boy of mine, so smart at some things it frightens me. This one was self-published and how often does one grab that off? And he told me that Mr. Clark held the book in his hands just before he died. Doesn't my Larkspur mix in some great company? My Larkspur."

She ably and without pause summarized that commendation with a bit of body language that more women understand than men, at least those women gifted with the language of the body and a kinship with the written word, and that includes all the 'Hallelujahs' or 'Oh, Gods' you can imagine at one and the same time.

From the very beginning Larkspur had said, very directly, that he was useless in the mechanical or electrical vein, especially to Katherine in their courting days. The up-front admission, he had discovered, kept him out of some impossibly embarrassing situations. Now, twenty-two years later, two sons in the house with a younger daughter, his balm and serenity for long spells of time undamaged, unapproached, unassailed, Katherine had left with the children for a benefit golf outing. Larkspur, not good with golf clubs either, was content to sit home and read, manage his stamp collection, now worth a considerable sum, or "coasting along," as Katherine was apt to say if questioned on his whereabouts.

"The plunger," he announced in a surprised aside, walking up the stairs. His voice bounced off the walls like a court dictate or spoken from a podium. A striking revelation!

"Of course, the plunger." It made his blood tingle.

Such a simple contraption could produce immediate results. A sense of glee came on him, an aura of knowledge and finessing and acute appreciation for the small things in life. Again, he said it, in that podium voice, his blue eyes lit up, his round pleasant face cracked with a smile; "The plunger."

His head nodded in agreement. Katherine would wonder how he had managed to get rid of such a pesky problem. And in such short order. Aha, that was the secret; do it in short order. In the air as promise sat the aroma of his next cup of coffee, French Vanilla, a little exorbitant, but it was a day off. In his hands, as if at order, would soon be the copy of "Notes from A Small Island." Today he'd finish that snappy little book and be on to City of Lost Maps, if that was its real title. He enjoyed the momentary doubt. It was not important, except that it was 'there' waiting for him. Now would be the important stuff, clearing up a small problem in jig order. "Aha," he announced again, the dais of the final step under his foot, "The plunger!"

Lo, that plunger would not budge even a half-pint of water. Not a spoonful! Larkspur plunged and plunged and heard a throat of a bubbling sound and saw small bubbles rise, but the water stayed in the bottom of the tub. Once, plunging so hard, his glasses fell into the tub. Putting them aside, he took off his shirt, and plunged again, with steep exertion. Nothing moved except a few bubbles. Their throaty sounds he heard from the innards of the tub, some kind of mesmerizing code behind the wall where things lay hidden, pipes and tubes and other chance things, the things in life one must accept.

Again, he plunged and breathed hard and thought of jig time and quick time and rapid solutions flying out the window.

For a long period, he sat on the hopper, John Crapper's masterpiece for casual reading, and thought about it all. Katherine was sure to bring boys home with her own. It was her way. She loved people, loved them underfoot, loved to feed them and sew for them and minister to little needs. God, she loved him under foot. It was her way in the world. But they would need to use the shower. She wouldn't let them or want them walking about smelling like a locker room. Katherine could not abide that.

He plunged again! Nothing but a solitary throaty bubble. It sounded as if it had come up out of his own throat. Again, he sat, and suddenly, with a flare, remembered an old-time actress on TV doing a commercial for some kind of magical liquid that took care of drains and such. Hair be damned! He'd get some of that. He was connecting!

Back in his shirt, his glasses on, going down the stairs, he saw himself pour a red solution down into the drain. He could hear the sounds as it sucked the tub dry of all its water. It was now two hours since Katherine had left. No longer did he have all day. Memories, in bold leaps, rode on top of his predicament, sweeping him up with connection, the plunger and the blockage serving as connectors. One dear friend, in clear affinity had said, "My favorite tools are the plunger, super glue, and duct tape." Oh, how well he knew that stance. They were kindred souls in that dark order of ineptness.

As he got into his car, he remembered another dear friend's relating a one-way telephone conversation he'd overheard in a doctor's office. "No, Ma'am, I'm sorry. If he had a stone up his nose, penicillin wouldn't remove it. By all means, if he wants to hold his breath until he's twenty-one, that's okay by me. No, Ma'am, I don't mind if you get a second opinion. I'm only one of the three best eye-ear-nose doctors in the world. I had my own hospital in Hungary until the Russians drove me out." Pause-pause-pause. "Who? Who? The guy in the gas station! Well take him to the goddamn guy in the gas station!" There was chuckle and relief always at hand. Panic always left openings for being overcome.

He drove to the small local hardware store that seemed to swear by kindness and inventive solutions to everyday problems. He explained to the woman at the store about the shower and Katherine's supposition of hair plugging the drains." "I have three daughters," the woman said, "and hair can do that. Try this stuff and it will cut right through all that hairball stuff." Her smile was wide and warm and well informed. And the liquid was red, just as he dreamed from some other life, and did nothing for his problem. For what seemed hours he sat there waiting for the chemical battering ram, waiting for the gurgle, the escape of tub water. Knowing he shouldn't do it, he plunged again. Nothing.

Panic was coming. He couldn't call a plumber and expect him to be here before Katherine and company. He tried a bent coat hanger, a thin wire coat hanger. It wouldn't go past the first bend or the obstacle that was more than a hairball. Looking the situation over once more, he discovered the small door behind the shower panel. To his mind it had never been opened. It was as about as mysterious as it could be.

Larkspur opened the small door gently and saw the pipes, the mass of pipes. Copper pipes. PVC pipes because they were white. Pipes coming and going, he presumed. One pipe was higher than the others. The drain from the bottom of the tub was connected to it. It rose well above the drain and was connected to the overflow outlet near the top of the tub. If he took that off, the coat hanger would certainly pass down through, past the connection from the tub drain. A new surge of excitement hit him. Using a screwdriver, he set about taking two screws holding the cap on the overflow connection. This was easy. He'd already got the cap off the drain in the bottom of the tub and not lost the screw. Now he placed two more two-inch screws on the floor and gently lifted the overflow cap from its place, taking it and whatever was connected to it from inside the overflow.

Whoosh! The tub emptied in mere seconds, the water and the red chemical liquid all gone in one Whoosh! The red stuff gone. It was as if his blood had emptied out! His energy! His dreams! Oh, the grand art of maintenance! Oh, salvation! The tub emptied. The drain, the damn drain, clean as it ever would be. Looking at his watch, he quickly with newly adept fingers put all the screws and caps in place, including the plug, now in the open position, which had kept all the damn water, and indeed the splash of redness, inside the tub.

Then he heard a horn blow a series of blasts, then blast again. Somebody, he interpreted, had made a hole-in-one. Larkspur smiled. So, had he. He wasn't the one who had shut off the drain outlet. Katherine's problem was solved. The electric and gleeful surge hit him again, Larkspur at ease with the world anew.

Lyrical Vacations North of Boston

Great vacations leave images that carry on for years, the imprints so indelible, so easy to recall when new chapters are to be written as we venture north from Boston, up the coast, over the hills, climbing the spine of the Adirondacks, to lakes, isles, sands, the grand hills and peaks calling for attention. They whisper to me from many points and in numerous ways, in music, in photos loose in my head, from faces and personalities befriended but if for short spells and long hereafters, from small excitements that have not been fully extinguished, that might never be extinguished.

On this graveled morning, wind and wire have become quick partners in Down East melodies, violent stretch of voices, cloud-high reach of their alphabet, and rare Elis hurled above October's crackling grass. Raw cries come ambivalent in outward leap from fence wire stiff as an immovable idea, and wind, moody as arias of grand operas or transient as hobos or gypsies from the arch of Time, touch me where mornings seep inward, the way forgiveness moves, slow mounting of steps, crunch on crunch, and then the not quite so simple knocks at my door.

Maine sun-ups need no introduction to what they toss about, placid as icebergs, slow and enormous, yet fit your mindset dependable as old gloves you've broken in, or a hunting jacket hanging beside the back door, a wallet pawed for years on end, or a hammer whose handle knows your palm with its unspoken and curved intimacy.

Mornings whistle, cause covenants with outlandish trees, quick rivers holding deep breaths, and along the hectic coast, blue stones trembling all day long, trembling, in the hush of music underfoot.

For sure, in rich recall, Hermit Island, Maine comes in swift return when I walked in night's syrup down a Hermit Island road, caught between snoring and 3 A.M. loving, waiting for the fish to wake. I felt the heat of stars and sand's abrasives, the mad interplay of elements thrusting at moccasins and eyes where, ahead of me, the moon pushed light's broad blade down through the perfection of trees, a leaf scattered its delight, a late moth struggled toward the infinities. I drank my cup, remembering a starfish caught hours before on a burst of rocks, its five fingers searching, as my senses did, for momentary salvation, that moment of vacation significance when I realized I had no enemies, I had no hate. I moved out, into, and was alone, with the grace of stars and the glitter of sand.

You vacationers understand such things change your voice, your outlook, your recall. The simplest things stand up for notice, attention, and the sharing of earlier times, other times, in one's life. Sometimes they are as simple as apples shared on the route of a solitary day, as you see how they've made the last run, like fire engine-red Macintosh, under batter with cinnamon, gone off to day school on yellow buses with brown-baggers, or bruised to freckled taupe and plowed under for ransom and ritual, their short lives crushed for one Thanksgiving cup.

Once, remembering such impact, I stood on a friend's home site, on the stiff lawn down-wind of winter, where I dropped first the first cold moon of a November into fractured wheels of apple limbs and heard the bark beg away from touch, or a pine ridge, catcher's mitt thick, grabbed winds riding off Rangeley, squeezed out cyber cries hanging red pendants on necks of new stars afloat above me, demanding attention, their slow crawl measuring a last vacation night for me. That's surely when midnight skies invoke my serious consideration of color, a reach beyond belief, new silent music, necklaces of astral proportions fit for knotting out over a choice Atlantic surge, blue, wishful linkage working at my level, past passage coming from the bogs I trod at my honeymoon, at hers, where memories made their start.

On one such evening, I saw boats sit at a river's mouth, their bows scattered as compass points, small scoops on an interminably huge sea rising to the ever imagined yet illumined line of sight where the gallant sailors fell off the known world. Those boats were not deserted, though faintly cold for oarsmen who walked down this beach behind me, stomachs piqued and perched with wine, salted hands still warm with women, mouths rich of imagery and signals. Their sons are left who later come down this beach to these small boats topping the Atlantic, gunnels but bare inches from the Father of Oceans, coursed to the stalked anchorage by thin ropes and a night of tidal pull. Here I stand between commotion and that other, silence; inhaling spills of kitchens, olla podrida riding the ocean air with a taut ripeness, early bath scents, night's soft dreams peeled and scattered to dawn, and see boats move the way sea and earth move against a distant cloud.

I question hammer and swift arc that drove pared raw poles of their moorings into the sea floor, picture a mustachioed Latin god laughing at his day's work while waving to a lone woman on the strand; and see her, urged from kitchen or bed, in clothing gray and somber, near electric in her movement and scale of mystery, eye the god eye to eye. Such is the mastery of eyes.

Inland, before dawn hits, an oarsman, tossed awake, knows an old callus where the Atlantic sends its swift messages, for up through toss of heel and calf, through thew of thigh and spinal matter, radiant in a man's miles of nerves, these small boats, gathered there, tell of their loneliness.

They all say such memories linger, depending on choice, location, that northern leap.

I Don't See Too Many Guys in Suntans* Anymore

*(U.S. Army Class A Summer Dress Issue, '40's-'50's)
You know, the old summer Class A's they saved
from their promised long weekend leaves,
those killers, those formidable young warriors,
those hot Omaha Beach swimmers with salt
in their noses and into gun barrels and curing
half the ills and evils they had ever known
as if it were the sole balm from the living god,
those St. Lo low flyers of updrafts of gray dawn,
Bastogne Bullies, bridge-wreckers at Germany's
inevitable edge; friends who passed through my
Seoul immemorial times leaving their footprints
for my wayward boots to overshadow, fill in,
pass on to this destiny. Of course, they have
popped the beltline button, split the crotch
in hell's anxieties, let their quick waistlines
go fallow with beer and dreams' nutrients,
those old warriors of Sundays past without
other balms, or Saturday evening shelling or
unconsumed bombs that threaten Wednesdays
fifty years later; those slim-legged survivors
who later wore them with collegiate jackets,
myriad sport coat ensembles, with slick-cigarette,
a crew-cut, such old world-in-the-face looks
that should have toppled their young empires.

You know them, how they came back to play
on the green fields as if they had never left

the chalk-striped confines, showed the kids
how the game used to be played, those sun-
tanners hitting behind the runners, bunters
of the lost art when the whole world sat back
on its heels that the big sound was now over,
put their muscle on the line late in the game
when the only thing left was heart and horror
at losing, having seen too much for their time.

Remember them on baked diamonds of the quiet
Earth, how there was an urgency to collapse
time into a controllable fist, yet how free they
were, breathing on their own, above salt water,
the awful messages buried behind their brows
for all time to come, unstitched wounds and scars
amber in late evening's breezes, like chevrons
from their elsewhere. Their only true badge
were the suntans carried home from Remargen,
Mount Casino or Inchon leaves, those slim, fit-all
occasion trousers, pressable, neat, signatures of
angst and annihilation and world freedom;
those narrow-waisted emblems of the Forties,
the Fifties, neat with tie and shirt, wore cement
on summer days of their labors, or roofing tar,
some to class and some not, collapsing time again.

I write this to celebrate the last Monday in May,
the day when the soft-shoed parade passes through
the middle of town and the middle of memory.
The hawkers will sell their bright wares, wearing
their municipal permits as badges, cylindering
balloons, authorizing plastic toy gun purchases,
leaving their remnant discards in cluttered gutters

the early sweeper will gather, making money
on the sad memorial, dreaming of next Flag Day
and the Fourth of July. Popcorn will burst
its tiny explosions, ice cream bars will melt,
children will think they gambol in a ballpark.
Then, then only apparent, I will see some old
ball players, the Earth-savers, underground or
remembering, chino-less and walking among
the very memorable names; comrade, comrade,
comrade or one's teammate, teammate, teammate,
illusions of the noisy past, clad in somber pin stripes
or cedar, carrying grandchildren, bearing them up
from under grass, evoking Monday of all Mondays,
those swift ball hawks, those young Earth-dreamers,
who survive in so many ways, that legion of names
falling across Saugus the way we remember them,
like a litany of summer evenings full of first names
gone past but called for the First Sergeant's roster:
Basil P., Thomas A., Lawrence D., Edward M., Guy C.,
Hugh M., Arthur D., Edward D., James W., John K.,
Walter K., William M., Frank P., Howard B., names
that settled softly called, reverent even for this day,
across a sun-drenched Stackpole Field, bat on ball
and the echo of a thousand games swung about the air
as if time itself has been compressed into late innings,
those swift ball hawks in pursuit of the inevitable; oh,
young, in May, the whole Earth suddenly gone silent,
but bound, bound to build memories, in May, in May.

V for Victor

I saw it all, from the very beginning, heard it all, too, every word rising on the air ... in our first classroom, in church, everywhere it happened, you name the place and I was there. Unannounced it came. From the heavens it must have come, taking over his soul, his body, his mind for a few bare minutes of magic. Once, and once only, every five year like clockwork, it came on him, as if grabbed by the heavenly spheres or ignition itself lighting up his lungs from the inside. My pal Victor, classmate for 16 years of schooling, teammate for 8 years, inseparable companion, fifth year custodian of miracles that made him, for the nonce, an extraordinary singer without explanation, an indescribable tenor so gifted I have to place the cause on an element beyond us mere men.

V for Victor, dit dit dit dah, dit dit dit dah, dit dit dit dah.

I never saw the miracle coming, in any of the situations. Neither did he, but it took hold of him and wouldn't let go until the last word fell from his lips, from his throat, from his lungs, and to depart then forever from him. No song was ever repeated, making the miracle even more mysterious, as he could not even recall the scenario within a half hour of it happening.

I often thought I hoped I'd be there when it was over. Or maybe I didn't hope so. It'd be sad enough to hear the last of it, knowing at that moment he'd be gone before another five years had passed.

You think I'm off my rocker, I'll bet, but I'll tell you I have not missed a word. Not that I was clued in on the moment of coming (I rarely knew it was coming until I was out of college and back home for good) and then the math of it hit me. So, because he was my best friend, because he was so loyal in his own right, a trusted teammate, a productive teammate, a leader, I started keeping a journal, plotting the next revelation, the next miracle.

His musical renditions were all glorious, out of this world, infused with so much talent it shook me. Perhaps it was a part of his emotional and physical make-up that brought up a message from within, carried it off so it could be shared. There just had to be something in the air, surrounding him, waiting for his hand or eye or lung to breathe it in so it could be let loose.

The time it happened when he was 15 years old, and not the first time I had been a witness, was the first time I thought his surroundings or the company he shared dictated his revelation, his sharing, his improbable gift. It was as though it was needed, not by Victor but by those about him.

I tried to trace that import from the third incident.

We were sophomores in high school, and every Wednesday evening, five of us, all teammates and classmates, would gather at Phil Barbanti's house where his mother fed us the ultimate in Italian meals. She and her daughters loved to cook, to feed us and her son during the football season. The good old smells of rich sauce were deep and delicious and flooded the house, all the rooms, the hallways, the bathrooms, probably the cellar and the attic, calling on the appetites, not letting go until cake or pie hit the table.

Mr. Barbanti sat at the head of the huge table partly in the kitchen and partly in the dining room where it was extended to accommodate we weekly guests, with a jug of wine, an old cider jug, in place beside his chair ... a deep, delicious Dago Red he called it, made in his own garage from his own grapes off his own backyard vines, a recipe from Italy come by boat fifty years earlier. That Dago Red, barreled in the garage, was often a target for theft of a pint or so, late at night, Barbanti house lights all dimmed or shut off, the four of us pals mischievously out on Saugus town.

Heavy, Buhda'd in his chair, the classic icon of the East Saugus Italian community, stonemason, violinist of sorts, warm as sin, Mr. Barbanti, by habit, often by choice, talked to his wife in beautiful Italian, almost musical, as if it had come directly from La Scala. I loved to hear him speak, sonorous at some moments, secretive another, yet a tenor's carry in his voice. I dreamt about learning Italian, but did not follow through with my intent. I think the result is the way I listen to opera now, putting in my own words for those being sung, making my own dreamscapes, composing my interpretation of an aria.

When Mr. Barbanti spoke, all commotion in the kitchen stopped, kettles stopped singing, pans stopped banging and clanging, glasses and plates stopped clattering. Sentences stopped in mid-statement as if a gavel had smashed down on the countertop. "Angelina, that sausage will be the best ever served in this room, I am sure of it," as interpreted by his son in a low whisper, and the order it indefinably contained, would be understood, the tone set for the evening, the feast ready for us princes.

So, it was on that night, the table cleared, a hum in Mr. Barbanti's throat coming musically across the room, a tune from old Italy most likely, that the ignition started in Victor's chest. The younger people in the house that evening were in the hallway to the upstairs, set off to the side of the kitchen, some sitting on steps, a couple standing, all gabbing, comrades at ease, sated, our mouths in a sweet and sour taste after being curried by meatballs and gravy and the inevitably delicious strawberry shortcake, when Victor stood up at the foot of the stairs, at attention to an invisible order, unsaid direction, with no outward sign, no outward expression, no full giveaway on his part. An alertness was telling me I was again to be witness to the miracle only he could accommodate. It was likely a moment, I was sure, that Victor did not know was coming, from wherever it was loosed, from what housing or crucible or dais where it was issued, as if on demand to be a living moment of time.

It came in Italian, rich as Naples I'd guess, abruptly, suddenly, rising from him who could not speak Italian, who could not read music, who had not sung a song, unknown to him but a few seconds before, for the previous five years. Instantly I remembered the last time, when he was ten, when I was once again at his side in such a situation, and here I was once more, right there in front of him as the unmusical Victor, grabbed by an unknown power, unknown force, unknown capability, unknown talent, broke into a song I had heard a hundred times but never from Victor ... never before from him and, as time would prove, never to come from him again.

He sang about what a wonderful, beautiful day it was: but it came in the Mother Tongue, La Scala powered, as beautiful if no more beautiful than Caruso himself:

Che bella cosa è na jurnata 'e sole, he sang, sonorous, rising up the hallway and through the whole house, *n'aria serena doppo na tempesta!* It was majestic, soaring, tilted the whole house on an edge. *Pe' ll'aria fresca para gia' na festa...Che bella cosa na jurnata 'e sole.* Eyes opened wide *at 'o sole mio.* Mouths agape at a boy singing in Italian who knew no real Italian other than a few curses, how to greet the day, say hello or goodbye, say supper was late.

Ma n'atu sole cchiu' bello, oi ne', 'o sole mio sta nfronte a te! 'o sole, 'o sole mio sta nfronte a te! sta nfronte a te!

A glorious song it was from the first note to the last note, a glorious sound loosed in the house, probably the first time ever the words rose in such incredible beauty within that brick house now set with fantasy or mystery. I had no name for it.

And heavy, chair-bound, stunned by beauty, Mr. Barbanti rose from his seat, his eyes also wide in amazement, a huge smile beginning on his face. "*Mama mia*," he said a number of times, and again as the song was finished, as Victor turned slowly, shaking his head in his own sense of wonderment, wondering again where this power had come from, this sweep of energy that came up out of him, this talent beyond measurement, this music and these words he had never known, and him also suddenly knowing he would never sing this song again as long as he lived. That knowledge must have also come to him from some distant place, must have been understood.

"You've been holding out on us, Victor?" Mr. Barbanti said. "All these times at dinner you never sang such a song, such a beauty of a song, and in a voice only the Maestro would own. I never knew you could sing. My God, son, do you know what this house has heard tonight? What I have not heard since I left Italy and my one night in La Scala, night of forever, Caruso out there in the light by himself, and that glorious voice raising the very heavens. What else do you have hidden? What songs hide there? Do you know *la Donna e mobile?* The Barber of Seville?" *Turondo? Sorrento?*" He must have known something else, been aware of some secret of the ages, because he blurted out, "Quick, son, before it is gone. Before the words go away." Had he been witness himself to such an outburst before? Had such a dream been realized in his presence, or by him, in that old Italy of his, the Italy rich with the glorious tenors, for now he had been in the presence of another magnificent voice?

And I knew exactly what was going to happen, as it happened before, five years before and five years before that ... Victor fled. Out the door of the Barbanti house he flew, down the street we saw him go, as if he was at Manning Bowl and the goal line was all of 80 yards away. Flew, he did, into a kind of reclusion where the upstart evening might somehow be put in a proper place of mind, if such a place existed for him. I doubt that it ever did, for on the following day he'd have no memory of the happening. There would be no note left hanging for him to hear (being tone deaf to begin with), no single article of his delivery, no reception remembered. A song would come and go, and every five years of his lifetime, as I had come to measure them.

It was his destiny, his fate, his mystery. I was the chosen observer.

The huge smile slowly leaving his face, wonder beset by awe and deepest curiosity, Mr. Barbanti said, "What happened here? Did I really hear what I just heard? Tell me what I heard. Please, somebody, explain it to me. My God, where did Victor go? Why did he go? Something is terribly wrong here or terribly right, but it's all amazing. What have we seen, or heard? I am not alone in this, am I? Did you not all hear it?" He stood beside his deep, comfortable chair, a man up from his throne, caught up in wonder a young man had freed in his house. "Mama mia," he said again, "Blessed Mother."

He seemed happier than he might have ever been in his whole life.

His wife and daughters were still speechless in the kitchen. Not a glass tinkled during the whole song, or yet. Not a clatter of a pan, though Angelina, the 14-year old, said boldly in her eyes she had fallen in love at the moment. "Yes, Papa," she said, "like The Gloria."

Still standing, amazement yet written all over his expression, he pointed at me and said, "He's your closest pal, Tom, right? What do you know?" Unwavering, steady as a post, he waited an answer, his eyes beginning to get red, and a story on his face.

I tried to explain it to him, and to all the others, though mysteries like this, or miracles, were things I did not handle well myself. "I first saw it happen in kindergarten. Victor, never having joined in a song that I can remember, suddenly one day stood up from a circle of little green chairs we sat in and began to sing a song called, I think, My Dog Blue. It was beautiful, so beautiful, that for three or four weeks the teacher, inviting the principal and the music director into her classroom, tried to get Victor to sing the song again. It never came back to him. He never knew a word of the song, even though he tried. It just would not come back to him from wherever it had come from in the first place." I paused, trying to remember some feeling I had back then. "They pushed hard at it, all of them. One of them finally must have said, 'Maybe we push him too hard. Let's sit back and see what happens.' It just went away after a while."

From the kitchen, a dish towel still in her hands, Angelina said, "Nothing ever happen after that? Once I heard about a boy in the Armitage School, in West Cliftondale, who sang a song at recess that brought the neighbors right out of their houses, and the teachers from inside the school all tumbled into the schoolyard to hear the boy sing one song. I don't know what that song was, or the boy's name, but I'll bet it was Victor." Her eyes flashed their new-found joys again, as if she was laying claim on Victor for evermore.

"Were you there, Tom?" Mr. Barbanti said. Did you hear that one too? What was it, the name of the song he sang that time? Do you know what's going on with him?"

"I was there," I said. "That time he sang a troubadour's song, in the old Irish, I guess. I don't think anybody in the schoolyard knew any of the words, but later on I heard that Mr. Dineen, the retired mailman sitting on his porch across the street from the schoolyard, was crying all the time, sitting in his old chair, his chin resting on his hands on the porch railing, just crying his eyes out. And they said he had been here for more than fifty years."

Mr. Barbanti said, "That's his piece of the miracle of this young man of ours, Tom. I wish I could have been there to hear that one. So, the Maestro doesn't own him outright, does he? What a pity. Nor La Scala herself. What comes after this? How will you know where to be, if you go to different schools, take jobs in a different place, how will you be at his side? You are fated, I assume, to be the only one to be in all his outbreaks, if I can call them that." The weight of him was deep into his chair, but he was uncomfortable once more, his face still shining with glistening curiosity, searching out causes and explanations.

He stood again, preparing to put a demand into the air. "You keep me advised on what happens to that pal of yours. Make sure you tell me. If you ever get a clue on the next time, tell me." The king had spoken beside his throne, the echoes undoubtedly ringing yet in his ears.

Thus, I departed under oath that night to keep him informed of his personal La Scala tenor, if and when I would still be privy to such an undertaking, my calendar marked for five years hence.

We left his house that night, the season over on the weekend, and never went back; Phil hurt his back in an accident a few months later and never played ball again. We drifted apart after that, except for Victor and me. And five years to the day, in church one Sunday morning, at the altar, the priest said, "Please be advised that Peggy has had a bad cold and is just recovering. Help her out if you can." His eyebrows were part of the announcement.

The procession started down the main aisle, Peggy singing. Obviously, her recovery was not complete. She sang terribly, a dissonance creating a stir in the church, not approaching a sense of music. The priest flinched at the altar at her feeble attempts. And Peggy, unable to let go, tried to continue.

"Oh, what is this?" Victor said to himself, as he sat beside me and something happened in his gut, at the back of his head, coming like an incomplete statement. He didn't know what it was, something breaking loose, coming apart, gaining its own force.

Again, I knew.

Then, in a crowning moment of some distant demand, he was jump-started like an old Ford or Chevie rescued from inertness; loose wires connected, a nerve touched into reality, a collection of breath taken in, and a stampede of energy loosed. One vein must have leaped across another vein. A nerve, twisted in the mix, lost its old harmony of things, its natural order, and found another setting. The new torrent came from a place he did not know in his body or in his psyche.

Victor stood up to help Peggy through the song. It was a revered hymn, one usually solemn and suddenly brought to heavenly acceptance, as Victor, my old pal Victor, began to sing, a most remarkable tenor, sonorous and golden-toned, operatic, like Pavarotti or Domingo or Carreras or blind Andrea Bocelli, a tenor the church had never heard. The priest cried at the beauty of the song. Peggy's mouth stuck open, an "Oh" caught up in awe. Every person in the church turned to look at Victor in the back row singing in that glorious tenor voice, everything freed from the fateful ignition, the magnificent torrent loosed from him.

It is five years later as I write this. I am in the Walter Reed Hospital in Washington. Victor and I joined the army two years ago. I went to Afghanistan, Victor to Iraq.

Accidentally, the pain in my legs determining my mindset, I just looked at the calendar. It's been five years since my dear friend sang one of his songs. The silence is deafening.

Receipt at Ogden's Twist

Young Trace Gregson, thin and curly at eleven and generally happy-faced, cringed whenever he saw Dirty Molly Sadow. If there was such a thing as a bad witch about in the world, she was it. People said her toes were black with earth rich as The Hollow, and that she smelled foul as chicken leavings.

Now Molly walked to the Amicalola River behind her little shack with a burlap bag in her hand. Her calico dress was rotten with age and stain and gray hair hung thin as tree moss on her shoulders. The beat of a limp was in her gait. Now and then the bag bumped along the ground as if the weight was too much for her to tote. Trace thought he heard muted cries coming from her side of Ogden's Twist, this torturous turn in the Amicalola River, as he hid in the weeds on the side across from Molly. One keeper trout flattened its rainbow inside his wicker creel.

Then it hit him. Molly's bitch of a Golden Retriever, Muscatel, had been full of pups but days before, her body low with the swelling. The soft cries came to him again, almost like prayers in the front row at church, and then Molly heaved the bag into the fast part of Ogden's Twist.

The bag hit with a big splash and sank in a swirl of current. Dirty Molly walked off without looking back.

Trace, in dungarees and sneakers, leaped into the river as soon as she went behind a mound of trash. The chill of the water hit him with a crushing blow. His breath held for him. On his second drop into the swift water, he found the burlap bag. His hand closed on the soft mass. The squirming in it telegraphed up his arm. Ashore, gasping for breath, he pulled the old shoelace loose from the twisted neck of the bag and dumped the contents in the tall grass. His eyes lit up. Life plummeted out! Five Golden Retriever pups spilled onto the grass. A sixth fell out and lay still. Trace felt his own heart bang in his chest.

Leaving the dead pup and his gear on the bank of Ogden's Twist, he rushed off to the most reliable and kindest man he had known in his short life, Uncle Jack Parlee, a retired mailman. Living alone, Jack kept a small garden on the river, this side of Ogden's Twist, a small garage notorious for its collection of old tools, and two old and labored hounds who were bent and slow in their years. Nameless, he simply called them my old boys.

As Trace knew it would happen, the salvaged pups were given a new home in a corner of the porch. The sun streamed in there at crazy angles at different parts of the day. Some days, by the rays, he could tell the hour or see his growth pattern on the wall. Trace could always sense the warmth of the porch. Jack promised nothing, but set straight away at continuing the salvage. He patted his nephew on the back of his head. "You got heart, boy. Momma did you good." Trace's father had died five years earlier in a late-night truck crash on the main highway west of the Amicalola. He and his mother now lived alone in their house.

Trace returned to get his fishing gear and to bury the dead pup. The sun was getting back a piece of his body, touching him reverently. For a brief moment he felt the thanks in it and the quick needles. A lone cloud sailed along at the bright horizon against Storm Mountain. He decided that at any second the cloud and the mountain top would collide. He'd be too far away to hear the crash. Still a long walk from his gear, he heard the howling and abated fury of a dog. For sure, he thought, it was Muscatel trying to reclaim her pups. At the banking of the river, Trace heard Muscatel's baying cry. It sounded like a friend's mother calling home her children just as darkness came filtering over the horizon.

Then Muscatel hovered around the trash pile behind Dirty Molly's house. Her nose was bent to the ground and she was howling weirdly. The noise caught up in Trace's chest. It made his heart beat with a new tempo. He felt as if he had just come up from another dive in the cold water.

Muscatel stood at the water's edge; her quandary evident to the sole onlooker. She stood as lonely as Trace Gregson had ever seen loneliness stand. The water moved swiftly, the beautiful Golden Retriever, like a statue, stuck her head into the air above the river. From where he sat in the reeds and tall grass, Trace believed she was measuring distance or possibility, or both. He knew he could not move her from that spot, could not drag her.

The cloud and the mountain went their way, silent and distant. The water of the Amicalola and Ogden's Twist, here and there turbulent, continued on its rush to the sea miles away.

Butterflies, though silent as smoke, punctuated the air against a deep green background of leafy trees, and the hum of bees and birds came as softly as a new engine.

The parallels slowly came to Trace Gregson in the days that followed.

"Them pups sure is pretty, Trace. Bet they grow like weeds from now on. Hate to have them loose in my beans and corn. They'd grow me under." His Uncle Jack sat on the rocker on the porch. "You keep an eye on that hag of a woman, that dog of hers, too, she ever leaves her watch. And if she gets fat again, you got more swimming to do."

And for weeks on end he saw Muscatel standing at the river, no longer baying out over the water, but watching, distance and possibility still crowding the air. Trace fished every day on his side of the river and thought about the widow's peaks his uncle had told him about that he had seen in parts of Maine and in New Bedford. "Lookout women waiting for their husbands' ships. 'Bout as patient as you can get," he said, "but needing a sure view of what was going on, what might happen. They plain last saw their man there, hoping to see him again at the same place." He thought the hapless mother would never leave her peak. Uncle Jack made no suggestions to that consideration.

It was months later, the pups sturdy as rocks, thick in the chest, bearing names he and Uncle Jack had conjured up out of a big collection of books, Trace saw the swelling again as it rounded Muscatel's frame. Soon after, he began a new vigil at the river. Every day he dug worms for the morning, saw Dirty Molly come evenings from the chicken farm where she worked, saw her off on the weekday mornings.

Rain had cooled the night. Morning was bright and leafy and green all the way to the mountain top. It was Saturday, his fly line floated down into the bubbling water of the river. Something in the air hit him broadside. It was the sound he had heard before, the near muted cries, the sense of loss or doom. Dirty Molly was making the same trip. On his belly, he slipped quietly through the weeds, his eye on her. Another burlap bag was in her hands. Again, it bounced on the ground. Again, it was heaved into the water. Again, she turned away and did not look back.

The cold water hit him again. His breath hung on again, but he felt a sudden panic this time. Nothing came to hand on the first or second dive. He dove a third time, his dungaree pockets now loaded with water, his sneakers heavy, his chest ready to burst. Uncle Jack would be on the porch with the dogs. The sun would be pouring down on them, sort of holy and secret and full of goodness.

He reached through the cold darkness, now desperate.

The bag touched his hands and seemed to loop away. He dove again and found it. Dirty Molly had wound a wire loop about the knotted neck. A point of wire pricked his thumb. The jackknife was in his dungaree pocket. He scrambled ashore, the bag instantly whipped out of water, the liquid film still crowding its surface, the whole bag sealed against breathing.

The knife was sharp and cut the bag easily and five more pups, spitting water, legs still at torment, spilled from the bag. As before, he put them in his creel and hurried off to sanctuary. He wondered how many of these trips he had missed in Muscatel's life, or in the life of any other dog that Molly might have kept.

Muscatel, as before, came again for days on end to the edge of Ogden's Twist. Trace watched her in secret as she sniffed the ground, sniffed the air itself, his own heart always in riot and commotion.

"Someday, girl, you'll have your day."

The two batches of kindred pups looped their harmony. Jack kept them in the yard, now with a fence around it. Though the garden was smaller, the dogs were bigger. One of his old boys had passed on and was buried at the edge of Ogden's Twist.

Some nights the porch for Trace was a piece of heaven.

Then one night, as the sheriff told it, someone had slipped into Dirty Molly's shack to steal the horde of money it was said she had hidden away. Molly supposedly caught him at it and died of a heart attack. There were no bruises on her.

But Muscatel was on her own.

One morning, his fishing pole over his shoulder and his creel braced with a pair of trout, Trace and Muscatel came together on Trace's side of Ogden's Twist, that adventurous spin in the Amicalola.

Trace had not seen her for weeks.

"C'mon, girl," he said, "we got some catching up to do." The two apparent strangers walked down the narrow road leading away from the river. The occasional trees overhead were umbrellas and loaded with warm sounds.

Trace Gregson knew the sun beating down on Muscatel and him was holy and full of grace. The back of his neck was warm. The warmth flooded his body. His hands felt it, and it went scurrying the length of his arms. He whistled. Muscatel, somewhat heavy-footed, trotted along beside him as if she were a long-time fishing pal. Jack saw them coming.

The folks at Ogden's Twist still say such a howling ensued that day that stories could be written about it.

Of Innocence and Reprisal

(or Ivan Stille Stuff)

I'll have to tell the story because I am the one most at fault here. I should have known better, I'm the new generation type. Even on the way home from the cemetery, going back to the house with my mother, my two younger brothers and my sister, it was me who should have known better. Lots of things should have tipped me off; instead of bigger, having more room with a body gone from it, the house was smaller. It felt smaller, it smelled smaller, the corners were tighter, and the air was cooler. I swore, after spending my first twenty-two years in it, it did not have its hand out for me.

My father's name was Ivan Stille. He was a writer of sorts, and once had been a Marine. The writing bit began in his late years. He had retired early; what had obviously built up in him for most of his life (us included) had somehow gathered into form and was finding a way out of the sepulcher he had devised over those years to hold his material. I don't know how many times I had heard him say to my mother, in those explosive years after he had found the computer, "Hey, Alice, you ought to read this piece I just finished."

He'd say it once, you could count on that, and then you could picture him waiting for the minute or so of silence. You'd hear the promise of exasperation from my mother, "There's plenty of time, Ivan. I've things to do now. I'll get to it bye and bye." There was sewing to be done, cooking, the work on her afghan for the Ladies Society. She didn't have a lazy bone in her body.

But then, in that small aftermath, a chair would creak, he'd swing it back in place in front of the computer, push a key, start again. That happened a lot of times those days. I can hear the weak echo of her words; I can hear the creak of his chair. All that day, all those days, he would not say another word, at least not vocally. It was the routine for most of the recent years. And there were so many mornings, before me and Teddy and Gus, and Janny last, had moved out of the house, that Ivan Stille, the late bloomer, the early riser, would be at the computer at three o'clock in the morning.

I'd come home for a quick visit from clear across the country. He'd beg me to make a CD of his material. It was, for me of course, a piece of cake. I did it in seconds. I did it every time I came home, which was at least three or four times a year. I never read what he had written. I was a technocrat, a new generation guy who loved the computer in my own way. It was not the memorial way of years that my father was carrying on with.

Teddy was a salesman and was damn good at his work. He came by every month or so, would stay for a few days in the old bedroom, do a few odd errands or maintenance chores, paint a hallway or wallpaper or hang some curtains, and move on. He was making lots of money and kept at it. Gus, driving his special bus for a big-time sports personality, rarely ever came home. Not even at Christmas. When he did drop by, there'd be a crowd of people gathering because they all recognized the big-time coach's bus, and Gus was able, in his own way, to get a few perks worked off for his folks. Janny had four kids of her own and tried, really tried, but it was tough to get home from Oregon where her husband Charlie, after years in the Navy, settled down. It was too expensive.

But, as it happened, none of us were readers. And we had all heard, growing up, some of the old gent's stories, Ivan Stille Stuff as we and some neighbors had come to call it, the pleasant parts of some late evenings on the porch or in the kitchen hunched over a few pops of coke or beer. It was old hat to us. And it was a shame that we had not listened more closely. But isn't that what we learn in life, and usually when it's too damn late.

So, the day came, and the day was announced with a thunderstorm and me in a plane and the captain sounding nervous. I promised I'd get home before the day was gone to say hello. The promise stuck. I came around the corner late at night in a rental car and saw the flashing lights of an ambulance and the companion fire truck. It was Ivan's heart. He didn't make a big race out of it. Just took himself into a final silence, and was gone.

All of us were there the next day, Janny coming last and Gus picking her up at the airport.

My mother made only one demand when we came back from the cemetery. "Now, while I have the help, get all of his clothes out of here and gone to Goodwill or the homeless of one sort or another. I don't care where they go as long as someone can get use from them." She added, as a small token of explanation, "It's what he'd really want."

We did all that in short order, did it in green bags and dumped them in a collection point. Useless, worn clothes and all kinds of underwear and socks by the dozens we threw out in the trash. Mom pushed us. "I don't have the hands I used to have. Nor the legs. It has to go now. Give those old coats and those jackets to the homeless. Every last one of them. Those old hats of his and baseball caps by the absolute dozens. His winter boots and fishing boots and his fishing poles. Give them to Harry next door. Give Harry his tools too if you don't want them. I'll never use them." She was practical, and realistic, down to the last handkerchief in one of his drawers, the last pair of pliers on a shelf.

That full day we moved as a team. The house, I'm afraid to say, started to grow again. Rooms leaped in size. Corners gleamed a gleam they had not shown in years. The cellar and garage grew themselves two or three times over. Space seemed to triple up in an hour's time. It was a kind of new-birth glory. It happened all the more every time a corner came back from where it had been hidden for years, and a one-time crawl space came exposed and a section of the garage she had never been in showed itself off.

Then, after all that acute labor had been expended on the house, to free up what one might call the debris of a lifetime, there remained only the small room he called the study. It was where his third-generation computer rode the edge of his desk, the one I had bought him and shipped home from one of my trips. His first computer was stuffed under a supply desk in a corner, its innards frozen for all time. The second one, one that I had worked on a few times and glimpsed but a few lines of his work, also went astray the day he got the latest one I sent, the one with the narrow console he thought was the next wonder of the ages. He had leaped at that one. I had made him CDs for of all his stuff. He told me he wanted a title printed on it. "Ivan Stille's Stuff Most Memorable." I had softly smiled to myself, loving his ideas, but not listening really... I was a CD maker, cut and dried! A tool merely. I knew my place in all of it.

In one corner of the room, in a closet, on packed shelves, stacks of papers had gathered and grown over the years. He must have spent all pre-computer days doodling on those papers.

Mom said, "What about all this stuff?" She looked at me for the answer.

I said, "He said it was all on the CDs I made. He had me transfer everything. There'd been a whole bunch of files. A whole bunch. I don't know how long it took him to do it all, but it's all on the CDs." I smiled, "We had about a dozen CDs. I made one of his whole system every time I came home. So much repetition, duplication, but he didn't want to miss a word."

The judgment was quick. "Get some bags, boxes, anything," she said. "Move it all. We can decode, decipher, read the CDs some other time."

We swung into action. The room leaped into life. Walls loomed in clear patches where piles of paper had hidden them for years. Teddy promised to paint and wallpaper his next trip. We moved a history of a man into bags and boxes and into barrels. We rushed. Mom kept looking at her watch. "It's trash day. It can all go now if we hurry." It was near three o'clock in the afternoon, destiny calling.

It was done. Outside the gears of the trash truck groaned in concert with weights. The grinding mill of its hydraulic gears swung the overhead crusher into the life-spill of papers. A piece of 8 1/2x11 paper flew on the quick breeze and landed in Harry's yard. He had been watching his friend being moved out. He picked up the piece of paper, looked at it, shrugged his shoulders and put it into his empty barrel. Toward the back of his house he walked, toting the barrel in one hand.

While the others were outside, watching the truck move away, I plugged the first CD in. There was one message. I have nothing memorable. The CD was empty. The same message came up on each of the twelve CDs. I have nothing memorable. I was shocked. Turning, I looked at the other computers. The emptiness fell down through me. The weight of years and piles of paper and powerful gears and awesome forces pushed down through my whole body. Oh, this awful retribution, this reprisal.

I knew. Oh, I knew. If I mentioned it to my mother, she'd raise a hand and say, "Today's not the day. Time for that later, in the bye and bye."

I heard the echoes. I heard the chair squeak; the key being punched. I didn't say a word. There'd be time for that later on.

It was four or five months later. I was heading out of Waylom Village deep in the tip of Michigan. I was passing a gasoline or oil truck with a flat tire. A small service truck was parked behind the big truck. Sun glinted on the bumpers. Two men were talking. The sun was also descending a hillside, tossing shadows aside. I could smell, not oil or gasoline, but honeysuckle or new cut grass or the edge of a barn's existence, a birthing of one kind or another. Perhaps it was promise itself.

A flock of birds was a small cloud against the sun, but only for a second. The radio was on and the man I occasionally listen to when I am in this part of the country was talking:

I swear I never heard his name before, but I know all of you will hear of it someday. I found these pieces in a new, small magazine. Some of the finest, grandest writing I have ever seen. We have to get this man here. We have to listen to what he says. It is most remarkable. It is brilliance itself. These three pieces are all I have. I hope I can get more. I hope I can get all of it, these things he called My Memorable Stuff by Ivan Stille. Does anybody out there know him? Call me at this number....

One Orbit Off

This star reconnaissance began on the fourth of July, the quick morning soft as a fresh bun, as warm, air floating up the stairs and coming across my bed in the smell of burnt cork or punk as smoky as a compost pile rising upwards from gutter and lawn debris the night had collected, spent rockets askew in gutters throughout town, clutter of half-burnt paper and tail sticks themselves once afire in night sky, signals giving darkness a new dimension of light and sound and the explosion of circular flares too bright to look at, as if the sun had delayed departure for the heart of celebration, as if stars had loosed their final demise amid or against the spatial junk they might encounter in outer reaches, the friction of them in the distance measured as silent as Indians in the past on these fields and paths at flint and rock, even as children younger than I was went secretly about the ways and quiet roads and lawns collecting expended shafts of excitement, rolling them into fisted quivers of their hands, tightly against their noses smelling residues of them, dross and dregs of sky-reaching powder short fires had implanted on their thin shanks as black as night was, so when fully amassed in one child's hand a match was re-applied in secret blaze of celebration began anew for those without money to buy their own pyrotechnics, the blue-red and orange-green flames loosed by this competition exceeding much I might have seen on holiday eve, these young scavengers, young army of excitement seekers like fresh winds adrift on the dawn, younger brother Charlie one of the aimless and directed searchers of ignited celebration goods; marked all the way across a vast lawn, where flags were hanging out all night, by his red hair and fiery eyes, even before the false dawn, his nimble legs in drive gear and nimble fingers at bundled grasp of sticks awaiting new flame; he, young Charlie, who was long ago appointed to the same bedroom as I, the choice between us as the one who would decorate the walls with Neil Armstrong's little dance down time's ladder and across the tempest tide of skies and blur of our black and white television set, this younger brother who dreamed and reached the stilted aerodynamics of lads, who exaggerated his heart and his mind for the unseen, the unknown, that far pit of darkness skies offer to imaginations leaping for the wonder of endless contact, sweet abrasions of the universe and its parts, coming global wanderer, aeronaut and astronaut and star traveler now out of the tight innards of the small bedroom Neil Armstrong carried on his back, the fiery-eyed, dreamy, celestial kid brother now in endless orbit and sending me these late signals from a far turn of the once-dark universe whose reception began in simple ignition beneath his hard fisted hand like a wondrous booster for his tell-tale heart.

The Humpty Dumpty Wall

The small hill was armadillo-ugly. An eyesore mound it was, a mound gouged up here behind his house many thousands of years ago, scored from the cataclysmic heart of Earth, and dumped in a major distortion by the Ice Age at a near-endless push. That energy, he envisioned, must have had a fire behind it, an upheaval of fantastic orders. So contradictory, the elements; fire and ice, the reach and retreat of glaciers, lava movement behind it all, Earth at slow rampage. Oh, it could make him shiver, such imagination. Then again, Craig Jolly thought the hill not unlike a whale out-Jonahed and pushed by an angry sea up onto the beach at Nahant, marooned, to rot unto oblivion as carrion.

He hated the hillock, yet wished he owned it.

One-time teammate Thad Brannock, a realtor, had an inveterate hunger for the land all about the area, and had at last taken the hillock (some thought it squeezed) from the old neighbor, Gregore Pazewski. For a long time Brannock had wanted the meager holdings of Craig Jolly; the half acre, the worn-looking Cape Codder Craig was born in, the small garden beside it just starting to break ground, getting April green. For years there had been differences between them, first as boys, then as teammates, and now, this far along in life, as men with families, men with destinies. Craig had often thought: We're so different, have different visions and memories that touch on other imagery, and decode unlike messages. If thought clouds, like in cartoons, were made graphic above our heads, they'd never match. Never!

His right leg in a cast from a ladder fall, Craig Jolly sat on his back porch looking at the ugly, sudden rise of land behind his house. If he owned it, he'd sure get it leveled, make two lots out of it, or more, whatever the building codes allowed nowadays. He'd bulldoze the highest part into the low portion just eastward; scrape with skill, he thought, his own Ice Age endowment. Someday sons Mark and Billy, at or near marriage, would have their own lots to build on, ones that would keep them close. It was another page, another color, of his imagination. Such things he was not sure of at all. More dreamy than investigative, more lucky than perseverant, was how he assessed himself at rare and chance occasions. The knowledge burdened him; that he could readily dream and project himself and the earth around him into distant and possible venues. Though he had trouble finding reality, he considered himself a realist. "Things are," he might have said, the odd moments in traction.

"Hey, dreamer, whatcha up to?"

The voice, from the top of the hill, was none other than the ambitious realtor. The bromidic turn of his voice was still in place. Though it posed an exaggeration, Craig knew the exaggeration would never go away. Thad Brannock, hands on hips, stood at the peak of the hill, looking down at Craig, at the small cottage, the small plot of land, the small garden stretched out beside the house, one small pimple in his vast plans.

Behind him, the purple of sunset scorched the Earth again, and made a silhouette as stark as Craig could imagine. Thad, he was sure, had waited on that moment of sunset, that time of drama. Even in cast silhouette, even in shadow Craig admitted quickly, Thad Brannock was thick through and through his body. Even in the perennial dark suit with slight vertical stripes, his shoulders were wide as sails, his legs like stanchions that once stood under the old Elevated in City Square and other parts of Boston. Strength appeared to have been poured from a Pittsburgh vat or from a cement truck's chute. As a fullback in high school, Thad had been a devastating blocker, but always announcing his major hits in the huddle before the next play was called, during the following week in the corridors at school, and later, much later, at Mulvey's Pub in the center of town. His memory of the make-up of those plays was prodigious, right to who had the responsibility of blocking who. His graphics and gestures were legendary, and colorful. Free drinks had always been at hand with discourse. Hack Mulvey loved to see him coming through the door of the pub, despite a slight hint of bile in his throat.

Thad, Craig had observed from the beginning, was very explicit in his moves and movements; always had the flair, a modern bard, a troubadour. Signals of a sort had always been a way with him, explanations accompanying the free broadcasts, the early notifications. Some men enjoyed that kind of communication. Some of Craig's pals called it pride. Others gave it sundry derogatory names, most of them bodily in origin. Yet he wanted to believe Thad was just checking out the territory where his two sons had begun to play, now and then casting a stone at his house, taking out a window one day. They had become, earlier in their lives than their father had, absolute pains in the butt. Craig's sons had definite instructions to stay far away from their activities, and had promised to make no amends for damages incurred. He would not have put it past their father, for the better of business, to instigate an edge of division, of separation.

"Hey, Craigie boy," Thad yelled, "wanta sell that little piece of heaven? Wanta do it now, I'll write a check right here and send it down with one of the kids." He chuckled loud enough for his old teammate to hear the chuckle. What he was saying was his kid Alex was going to be the starting shortstop on the Little League team, while Craig's son Billy was slated for right field, the kind of out-of-sight, out-of-mind position for weak hitters in the league. Billy was a weak hitter for sure, but there were trade-offs and other advantages that came leaping at him, other valid measurements.

Craig's father had once told Billy about tipping his cap to old ladies, and the boy remembered it on every occasion. That pushed him up in Craig's mental batting order, a No. 4 batter in life skills.

Craig gave Thad one curt answer. "Thad, you just make sure your boys keep their rocks to themselves when they're playing around up there." He felt strange saying it, feeling at a disadvantage, Thad up there on high, him down here.

"Hey, Craigie," Thad replied, one hand on one hip, the shadow thrown, "Boys will be boys, and these two of mine know where their throws go. They got the goods, both them. They just about do everything but drive the bus." His hands were on his hips, his head shaking in dramatic belief.

Two days later, and Saturday to boot, at exactly eight in the morning, birds were at a minor riot. The maple tree in front was full of what looked to be a thousand birds. Black as Hades they were, noisy marlins Craig assessed, a cloud settled on sprig and limb.

Then, with a sudden roar, he heard an engine kick start. The house shook right to the timbers. In one window a shadow lifted across the sun as he sat in the kitchen with coffee. He was not sure if it was a puff of black exhaust from a noisy diesel engine or if it presumed the thousand birds leaping into sudden flight. The engine roar, though, was not unexpected. Thad, with his town permit, had informed him he was going to build a retaining wall. A twelve-foot retaining wall. It would stare Craig right in the face, a mere fifteen feet from his house, almost atop his garage.

Thad, of course, had the right. Craig would have the shadow.

All morning the huge bucket shovel dropped into soft earth, swung bucketsful onto the side of the hill. A number of times the operator had to do a switch, finding room where gravel and loam from the footing displacement could be stored pending the wall's erection. The small green patch that was Craig's garden did not go untouched. The operator at each transgression shrugged his shoulders and looked up at Thad on the crown of the hill. Thad, still suited but wearing temporary site boots, shrugged back. All of it seemed pre-arranged; damage assessment would be small, Thad would take care of any problems, work on the footing would proceed at a pace, Craig would understand. After all, they were old teammates.

The machine had to snake closely around Craig's garage. The operator at one point shut off the engine and climbed down from his seated perch. He sought out Thad on the hill. "I'm a bit leery about that garage down there." He pointed at Craig's one-car garage. "Hell, one rock might drop it onto itself. For damn sure, if I bump it, it's going down. Must be a thousand years old."

"Don't worry about it," Thad had practically shouted, his voice carrying easily downhill. "If it comes to that I can rebuild it for a hundred bucks. Piece of cake." He thumbed the operator back to work. Craig, hearing about every word, admitted to one saving grace in the realtor; he had never once heard Thad Brannock curse any man or anything. It must mean something, he thought.

The work that whole day was tenuous at times; rocks rolling, the garden invaded by huge wheels, the invasion halfheartedly calculated to be noninvasive. Thad's sons scampered around the hill, at a game of sorts. They seemed to be at home near the heavy equipment, and their father somewhat oblivious of their activities.

Late in the day, the footing trench all dug, loam and gravel pushed back onto the hillside, a cement mixer truck rolled up in front of Craig's house. The logo said Wakefield Ready Mix in bright red letters. Thad yelled down to Craig, "I got this guy on overtime, Craig. Looks like I'll have to have him access the trench from your end, from down there. Too tough up here." He pointed over his shoulder. "That okay with you, old buddy? Save us a lot of trouble, both us."

Craig, fully expecting the move, nodded. It was the least of possible evils. The truck rolled into his yard eclipsing only a few plants, a minor stretch of grass. In a short effort the footing trench was filled to grade mark, the shovel operator leveling with a trowel the final surface. Truck and machine disappeared into the deep April-purple sunset. In the shadows, Thad gone, Craig could hear Thad's sons still at play somewhere on the other side of the hill. He left to pick up his wife from her volunteer job at the library. Change again, he realized, was at hand. Change was always at hand. The sunset was now a clear pinch of orange and pink, with a decent share of contentment.

Sunday evening, most things quiet, a small stone or pellet hit the side of the house. Craig and the boys raced outside but no one was in sight. A trail of sound limped into the darkness from beyond the hill, like a wounded animal making escape. Craig would not let the boys follow up the sound.

He also suspected that more was coming from Thad's end. It would be inevitable that the forms truck had to be unloaded in his yard, the work performed from there. When the forms trucks showed up on Monday morning, two of them, a knock came at Craig's front door. The driver said, "Brannock said we ought to talk to you about setting the forms up from your yard, if it's okay with you. Do our work from here. Says we have to clean up, make any repairs, he'll square things away for you." He looked around the side of the house and up the hill. "It'd be hell working from up there."

The driver had an honest look about him, generating an explicit plea to make his day easier.

Craig agreed, not making any demands, not exercising any rights. His wife Mona thought different. In the kitchen she said, "It's plain abuse from an old teammate who's just using you and your soft edge. God, the man makes me sick." Not with a huff, but with some pronouncement, she left the room. On the way out she offered her day's schedule, "I'm going to visit my mother. Be back at lunch. If not then, at least by 2:30 to get the boys to practice." He knew her as countable.

The parallel wooden forms to set the cement of the wall were all in place by noon, about sixty feet of plywood forms, heavily reinforced, with their smooth sides facing each other, were erected one foot apart. Craig saw the hard-working crew tie in steel rods holding the forms together. They also served as spacers, and a series of PVC pipes were also set at specific distances down between the wooden forms. The PVC would allow drainage to occur from the backside of the wall, once it was filled in, preventing hydrostatic build-up, a force he assumed as powerful as what might have formed the hill in the first place. The crew chowed down at lunch, spreading themselves against the garage in a minor noon shade. Craig could hear the stories of other jobs, Thad's name popping up a few times along with joined, risqué laughter.

On Tuesday morning the Wakefield Ready Mix truck returned, a monster in the early light, the huge barrel turning slowly. Two men from the forms company arranged the pouring of cement into the forms by chutes from the barrel of the truck. It went quickly and easily, without interruption. Little additional grass, and few of Craig's plants, suffered. The clean-up was complete and thorough. A small load of rich loam was shoveled off a stake truck, spread, rolled, seeded, and watered. The yard looked better than it had before the project started.

For four days the forms sat in the April sun, the cement setting in place, twelve-foot-high from the top of the footing, and a full foot thick. The forms men came back on the fifth day after the pour, broke the heavy forms down, and loaded them on their flatbed truck. The ends of the tie rods were snapped off on each side of the wall by a smash of a six-pound hammer. Deep Portland gray, not unlike a prison boundary, the retaining wall towered in the back yard. The openings of the PVC pipes looked like Cyclops eyes on the gray surface. All the forms were hauled away for future use. Division, Craig noted fitfully, was complete. The old dream of buying the hill, leveling it off, was gone. Soon, Craig also knew, there'd be a bigger shadow atop the hill.

Nights, with the mosquitoes in play, the random fireflies beginning to dare entrance, the peepers singing at the pond, Craig was not bothered by the wall he did not see. It could have been a hazy daytime illusion that night took away. Once in a while he could hear children's voices on the other side, at games, at tricks, their gaiety like songs. He could recognize the voices of Thad Brannock's sons. A full two weeks after the wall was poured, another machine came and backfilled up to the top of the wall. It was a small front-end pay loader and took much of the day to do the task.

A week after that the rains started. Rain came for four straight days. A lot of rain. Records were being unearthed, checked out. Part of Craig's garden went asunder, some portions of new grass went mushy. When the hydrostatic pressure became too great behind the wall, when the unknown hundreds of gallons of water collected in one earthly and powerful surge.

Earthly and powerful surge, the wall came down, bursting onto Craig Jolly's garage and flattening it, dropping tons of gravel and loam and mud onto his back porch, obliterating his kitchen. The town engineer and an insurance representative, upon investigation, found every one of the PVC drainage lines plugged with tennis balls that had been jammed into the openings. Earth had seeped in, had formed a formidable block, had set store.

Thad, of course, tried to blame Craig's sons, but nobody ever saw them near the wall. It was always Thad Brannock's sons at play. Payment, at last, came due to Craig Jolly.

Heaven and Hell Have Their Ways

A despairing writer died and was given the choice of going to Heaven or going down to Hell.

He decided to check out each site on his own, with Hell coming first. As the writer descended into those fiery pits, he viewed rows on rows of writers each one chained to their desks in steaming sweatshops, the whip lashes and groans loud and evident as they worked, and were repeatedly whipped with the thorniest of lashes.

"Oh, my, Oh, my," said the writer. "Better let me see Heaven, and right now!"

Moments later, as he ascended into Heaven, he saw rows of writers, chained to their desks in a steaming sweatshop. As they worked, they, too, were whipped with thorny lashes just as down below.

"Wait a minute, hold on here," said the writer. "This is just as bad as Hell!"

"Oh no, it's not quite the same," replied an unseen speaker, "here, everything gets published."

Made in the USA
Middletown, DE
25 October 2020